DANIEL

THE PRAYING PRINCE

TOLD BY CARINE MACKENZIE
ILLUSTRATIONS BY FRED APPS

Copyright © 1995 Carine Mackenzie.
Reprinted 2000, 2002, 2004 & 2007
Published by Christian Focus Publications, Geanies House,
Fearn, Tain, Ross-shire, IV20 1TW, Scotland, U.K.
Printed in China
ISBN: 978-1-85792-155-7
www.christianfocus.com

CF4•K
Because you're never
too young to know Jesus

Daniel was a fine young man, born into a noble family in the land of Judah.

King Nebuchadnezzar of Babylon led an invading army which defeated the army of Judah. He took away valuable treasures from the temple and captured many fine young men. One of his prisoners was Daniel.

The king selected Daniel and three of his friends to be trained to work in the royal palace. They were fit and strong and handsome. They were clever and quick to learn. A three-year training programme was started in which Ashpenaz, the chief official, taught them the new language. They had to read all the important books.

Daniel and his three friends loved the Lord God and served him. God was most important in their lives.

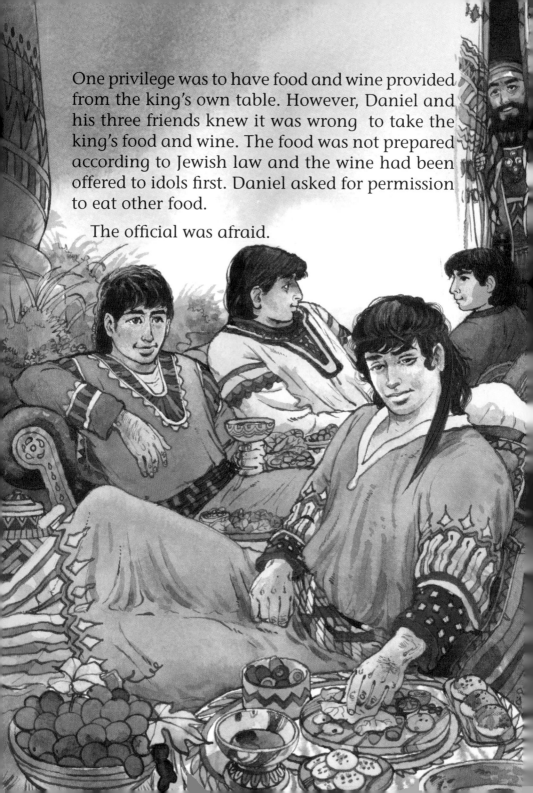

One privilege was to have food and wine provided from the king's own table. However, Daniel and his three friends knew it was wrong to take the king's food and wine. The food was not prepared according to Jewish law and the wine had been offered to idols first. Daniel asked for permission to eat other food.

The official was afraid.

'If you get thin and unhealthy,' he said, 'the king will kill me for not doing my job properly.'

Daniel said, 'Let's try it for ten days. Give us vegetables to eat and water to drink. Then compare us with those who eat the king's food.

After ten days Daniel and his friends looked healthier than the others. So the guard allowed them to keep to their simple diet.

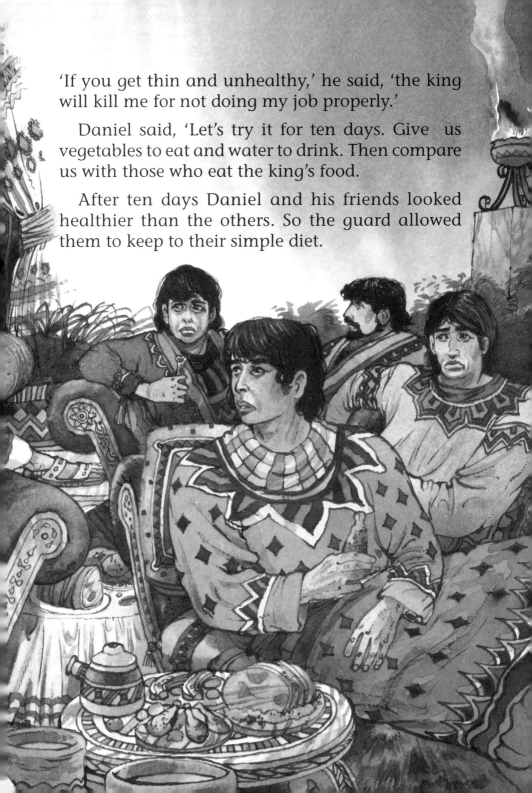

One night King Nebuchadnezzar had a dream, which worried him so much he could not get back to sleep. He called for his wise men and magicians to tell him his dream and its meaning but no one could do that. The king became so angry, he wanted to kill all his wise men.

Daniel heard of the king's cruel intentions. He asked him, 'Can you give me some time to try and interpret your dream?'

Daniel went home and explained the situation to his friends. 'Pray to God about this,' he urged, 'so that I can solve this mystery. If not, the king may kill us as well as the wise men of Babylon.'

During the night, God revealed the answer to Daniel in a vision. Daniel was very thankful. 'I praise and thank you, O God. You have made known to me what we asked,' he said.

Daniel went to the king's guard. 'Do not execute the wise men,' he told him. 'Take me to the king. I will interpret his dream.'

'Are you able to tell me what I saw in my dream, and to explain the meaning?' demanded the king.

'God has shown me this mystery,' Daniel explained. 'I am really no wiser than any other man, but God has used me to show you what will happen.'

Daniel told the dream in detail and explained its meaning.

Nebuchadnezzar was so impressed that he fell down before Daniel and honoured him. 'Surely your God is the God of gods and the King of kings,' he declared.

Daniel was promoted to be ruler over a part of the country. He was put in charge of all the wise men.

Daniel's friends were also given good jobs in the government.

After Nebuchadnezzar died, Belshazzar became king. He made a great feast for a thousand of his noblemen.

While they were drinking wine, he ordered the servants to fetch the gold and silver goblets that Nebuchadnezzar had taken from the temple in Jerusalem. They all drank wine from them praising their man-made idols. At the height of their drunken merriment, a strange thing happened.

The fingers of a human hand appeared and wrote on the wall near the lampstand.

Belshazzar was alarmed - his face turned pale, his knees knocked together, his legs collapsed.

What did these strange words mean? He called for his wise men, but they were all puzzled. The king was even more alarmed.

The queen overheard the uproar in the banqueting hall. 'Don't be alarmed,' she said to the king. 'There is a man in your kingdom who can solve the problem. Call for Daniel and he will tell you what the writing means.'

Daniel was summoned to the king.

'If you can tell me the meaning of this writing, I will give you presents and make you the third highest ruler in the land.'

'I do not want any gift,' replied Daniel. 'But I can tell you what the writing means.'

'You have set yourself up against God. You have misused the goblets from God's house,' Daniel told him. 'You do not honour God, who controls your life. So he has sent this message to you.'

These are the words which were written on the wall.

MENE, MENE, TEKEL, PARSIN.

This is what they mean:-
'Your reign will soon be at an end.
You fall short of God's standard.
Your kingdom will be conquered
and given to someone else.'

Daniel was given a beautiful purple robe and a gold chain was placed around his neck. He was made the third highest ruler in the land.

But that very night Belshazzar was killed and Darius from Media took over the country.

What God had warned had indeed happened.

Daniel was so highly thought of by King Darius that he wanted to promote him to be chief administrator of the whole land.

The other officials became jealous of Daniel.

'How can we find fault with him?' they asked one another.

But Daniel was completely trustworthy. He was honest and always did all his work.

'We will never be able to catch out this man Daniel,' they said, 'unless we can think of something to do with his worshipping God.'

So the officials hatched a plot against Daniel.

A group of officials went to see King Darius.

'We think you should issue a law, O King, saying that anyone who prays to any god or man except you during the next thirty days, should be thrown into the lions' den. Put it in writing, then it will be law.'

King Darius felt very flattered and agreed to do as they suggested.

Daniel learned of the new law. He knew that to obey it would mean disobeying God. It was more important to Daniel to obey God than any king.

Daniel went home and straight upstairs to his room. He knelt by his open window as he always did three times each day and prayed to God. He thanked God for his goodness and asked him for his help.

The jealous officials were looking out to see what Daniel would do. They saw him praying and immediately went back to the king to tell tales.

'Daniel did not pay any attention to your law,' they reported. 'He still prays three times a day to his God.'

King Darius was upset. He had not intended any harm to come to Daniel. How could he rescue him from the lions' den?

The officials would not relent. 'Remember the law issued by the king cannot be changed,' they said.

So the king sadly gave the order. Daniel was thrown into the den with the fierce lions.

'May your God, whom you are always serving, rescue you,' said the king to Daniel.

A big stone was placed over the entrance to the den. The king sealed it with his own signet ring and with the rings of his nobles.

How could Daniel survive this dangerous situation?

King Darius went back to his palace. He was miserable. He could not eat, he could not sleep. He did not want any entertainment.

As soon as it was light he hurried down to the lions' den. "Would Daniel still be alive or would the lions have eaten him up?" he wondered.

As he came near, King Darius called out nervously, 'Daniel, has your God been able to save you from the lions?'

The king was overjoyed to hear Daniel's voice reply. 'My God sent his angel to shut the lions' mouths. They have not hurt me at all.'

The king gave orders for Daniel to be lifted out of the den. He did not even have a scratch. He had trusted in God. God had kept him safe in such a dangerous place.

King Darius sent an order throughout the land. 'In all the land, everyone must fear and honour the God that Daniel serves. He is the living God. He has rescued Daniel from the power of the lions.'

Daniel put God first in his life. He loved and served him in every detail. He prayed to him regularly and trusted him to help him always. God loved Daniel very much and used him to speak his word to important people.

Do you love the Lord Jesus and serve him in all the details of your life? We should pray to him regularly and ask him to save us from the danger of the evil that could so easily harm us. The Lord is willing to save all who come to him by faith.